MEN-AT-ARMS SERIES

EDITOR: MARTIN

The Royal Navy
1790-1970

Text by
ROBERT
WILKINSON-LATHAM

Colour plates by
G. A. EMBLETON

OSPREY PUBLISHING LONDON

Published in 1977 by
Osprey Publishing Ltd
59 Grosvenor Street, London W1X 9DA
© Copyright 1977 Osprey Publishing Ltd
Reprinted 1990

ISNB 0 85045 248 1

Filmset by BAS Printers Limited,
Over Wallop, Hampshire
Printed in Hong Kong

The First Uniforms

For many generations officers and seamen of the Royal Navy were complete individualists when it came to the matter of dress. This often made two ships of similar construction appear entirely different when the crew was mustered. However, some degree of uniformity within a ship had been in existence for many years before the introduction of regulations, as the seamen were provided with 'slop' clothing, the cost of which was deducted from their pay. As early as 1623, it had been considered a necessity to provide 'slop' clothing to '... avoyde nastie beastliness by diseases and unwholesome ill smells in every ship'. The 'slop' clothing was put in the charge of the purser by the Navy Slop Office, which procured clothing and cloth by contract. If the volunteers or pressed men required clothing when they came on board they were allowed to buy some to the value of two months' pay and afterwards to the value of 7s per month if they could show need. Men who came aboard in rags, either from the press gangs or from the courts, were forced to buy clothing and bedding. Seamen generally preferred this method because it meant that they did not have to part with ready money. By the end of the eighteenth century, contractors supplied to the Navy Slop Office such items as white canvas kit bags, blue coats, waistcoats and trousers, chequered blue and white shirts, black silk scarves, thick woollen stockings and a large variety of other items.

The purser, for his trouble, received 5% commission on all sales from the contractor who sent the slops in to the Navy Office. Pursers, or at least the majority of them, were generally dishonest. They were not content with their shilling in the pound commission, charged more for slops

than the fixed price, and even sold slops to 'dead' men. (This entailed 'selling' clothing to a member of the crew who had either died or been killed in action. The purser simply altered the the 'ticket', the paying-off account, accordingly.)

A number of officers and others, including naval surgeons, realized that much could be done for the seaman's appearance and his morale if a standard uniform was issued, and surgeons pressed for this on health grounds. In 1757 Dr Lind, the first man on record to carry out controlled dietetic experiments, suggested that seamen

1. 'British Plenty' – a seaman of 1794 consorting with some of the inhabitants of Portsmouth Point. Note checked shirt, spotted scarf, and gilt shoe-buckles characteristic of shore-going rig worn by sailors lucky enough to get ashore with some prize-money to spend. (Parker Gallery)

2. **Master, in uniform of 1787–1807. The crossbelt plate bears a crown and anchor, the buttons an anchor. (National Maritime Museum)**

should be put in a uniform. In answer to the Admiralty's standard reply that as the men were paid off with their ship, it was not economical to spend money on uniforms, he added that '. . . this could be overcome by some little removable badges or variations by which it might be known to what ships they belong'. The Admiralty ignored the suggestion but did issue some form of hospital uniform – although in fact this was to stop patients deserting – and in 1795 an issue of soap was authorized. Again in 1777, a suggestion was made that uniform be issued with '. . . a small round hat with a narrow belt on which should be printed the name of the ship'. It was not until a hundred years after Dr Lind's suggestions that the Admiralty finally ordered a uniform for seamen.

Officers were also allowed a great latitude in dress until 1748, when an order was issued '. . . in Order the better to distinguish the Rank of Sea

Officers, to Establish a Military Uniform cloathing for Admirals, Captains, Commanders and Lieutenants . . .' Midshipmen were also included to give them 'better credit and figure in executing the commands of their Superior Officers . . .' These uniforms, with minor alterations, continued to be worn until 1767, when full dress was abolished. Full dress was again permitted for some officers in 1774, and in 1787 orders in the *London Gazette* authorized a new pattern which was being worn at the beginning of the Napoleonic Wars. The following brief details show the typical uniforms ordered:

Admiral, full dress: 'A Blue Cloth Coat, laced with Gold Lace, and Loops of ditto, on both sides regular; Three on the Flap; stand-up collar, with Three Laces; White Silk Linings; Gilt Buttons with small Anchor in the centre, encircled with a Laurel.'

Admiral, frock uniform: 'Blue Coat with Blue Lapels and Cuffs, Gold-Lace Holes, pointing at the End, with the same Disposition of them as before; stand-up collar with One Hole on each side, Three Holes on the Flap, Three on the outside Cuff, and Three behind; White Linings; New Anchor Button with Laurel, same as to the Full Dress.'

Captain, three years post, full dress: 'Blue Coat with White Lapels and Cuffs, laced with Gold Lace, the Pockets double-laced, round cuff with Two Laces; Three Buttons to the Pockets and Cuffs; Blue stand-up Collar double laced; White Lining; new Buttons with the Anchor in an Oval.'

Warrant Officer: 'Blue Cloth Coat with Blue Lapels round Cuffs; Fall down Collar; Three Buttons to the Pocket and Cuff, White Lining but not edged with White; Buttons with an Anchor, same as the Captain's former one.' With the coat, white waistcoats and white breeches were usually worn together with stock, shirt frill, sword cross belt and sword. The head dress is not mentioned but the cocked hat was worn either 'athwartships' or 'fore and aft' depending on the individual or the likes of the captain of a particular ship.

These uniforms, and others of similar cut and design for other commissioned ranks, continued until 1795 when new patterns were introduced. These changes affected the coat; the white waistcoat and breeches continued in use, and the head dress remained unchanged. The new regulations were again published in the *London Gazette*. The main alteration was the introduction of epaulettes, the discontinuation of the white facings, the return to the slash cuff and the use of arranged buttons to denote rank. From the regulations we see that a captain in full dress was ordered a 'Blue Coat with Blue Lappels and Long Slash Sleeve, as formerly worn:– The Lappels to have One Row of Gold Lace, and the Cuffs and pockets Two: Two Plain Gold Epaulettes:– White Lining; White waistcoats and Breeches; Gold-Laced Hat.' As will be noticed, the head dress is mentioned for the first time. Epaulettes were only to be worn by flag officers, captains and commanders, and rank was denoted as follows:

Admiral: Two gold epaulettes, three silver stars on each.

Vice-Admiral: Two gold epaulettes, two silver stars on each.

Rear-Admiral: Two gold epaulettes, one silver star on each.

Captain, Three Years Post: Two plain gold epaulettes.

Captain, under Three Years Post: One plain epaulette on the right shoulder.

Commander: One plain epaulette on the left shoulder.

Even though the regulation stipulated what was to be worn, individualism still cropped up. Admiral Jervis, Earl of St. Vincent was forced to issue an order in 1797 in which he complained that he had seen '. . . several officers of the Fleet on shore dressed like shop-keepers in coloured cloaths, and others wearing Round Hats with their uniforms in direct violation of the late order of the Rt. Honble. the Lord Commissioners of the Admiralty . . .' He went on further to say that any officer offending against this 'wholesome and necessary' regulation would be arrested and court-martialled and never allowed on shore while the officer served under him.

Besides the outright disregard of regulations, officers could still be individualists *within* the regulations, as there were no details of cut or measurements for the tailor to follow. A note in the pattern book of Welch and Stalker (now in the

3. Lieutenant, 1799. This gives a fairly exact idea of the dress of a junior officer at sea at this period. Published by Ackermann. (Parker Gallery)

Victoria and Albert Museum) mentions that 'Some old gentlemen have their lappels nearly as low as the waist, there being no particular order about that, it being regulated by the will of the wearer.'

The next change in dress occurred in 1805, when physicians and surgeons were given a uniform of their own rather than that worn by warrant officers. The order detailed a 'Blue Cloth Coat, with Blue Cloth Lappels, Cuff and Collar, Collar to stand up, Two Rows of Gold Lace half an inch wide round the Cuffs and Collar, Three Buttons on Pockets and Cuffs . . . plain Hat.' Surgeons wore the same without gold lace, but the addition of two embroidered button loops on the collar. No epaulettes were ordered, to the disgust of some surgeons who had previously petitioned for them on the grounds that their position should be in line with that of army surgeons, who wore epaulettes. The preoccupation with epaulettes was due to the Napoleonic Wars and the love of this item by the French. Naval officers who wore no epaulettes complained on numerous occasions that foreign soldiers and sailors failed to salute them. Even Nelson had referred to them as '. . . part of a Frenchman's uniform'.

The uniform race appeared to be on in earnest, for in 1807 the Masters of the Port of Chatham, spurred on by the uniform given to medical officers, asked for improved status and a uniform of their own, complaining that if they were captured they would not be treated as officers. Masters and pursers were accordingly given a uniform of a blue coat with buttons bearing the arms of the Navy and Victualling Board res-

4. The Press Gang on Tower Hill, from a cartoon by Collins, 1790 – showing, if somewhat crudely, the methods employed by the 'Press' to recruit for HM ships. (Parker Gallery)

pectively. The Navy Board button had, in a roped oval, a large single anchor with a smaller one each side. The Victualling Board button had two crossed anchors in the oval.

In 1810, permission was given to those post captains who had been appointed commissioners of the navy, Victualling or Transport Boards and had missed promotion to flag-rank, to wear the undress uniform of a rear-admiral with plain epaulettes and the button of the board on which they were serving. Two years later this permission was extended to include the governors of the Royal Naval Hospitals and the Royal Naval Asylum, and the lieutenant-governors of the Royal Hospital at Greenwich and the Royal Naval College at Portsmouth.

In 1812, an important change in the dress of Naval officers was sanctioned. This was the reintroduction of white lapels and cuffs for flag

officers, captains and commanders. Other alterations included the addition of a further lace stripe on the cuff to distinguish an Admiral of the Fleet and the granting of two epaulettes to all captains and commanders. The two grades of captain were distinguished on the strap by the senior captains having a crown and anchor and the junior captains having an anchor only. Commanders had plain epaulettes and lieutenants were granted permission to wear a single epaulette on the right shoulder. A new pattern of button was introduced with a crown above the anchor and cable. This pattern, with minor changes through the years, is still in use today. The only officers not to adopt the new button were gunners, boatswains and carpenters.

Some captains took great pains to see that their men were dressed in some degree of uniformity and Captain J. C. Roberts of the *Plyades* issued an order in 1814 forbidding the men to purchase '. . . any other cloathing than blue white or red waistcoats, blue or white trousers, black handkerchiefs and hats.' A further order laid down exactly the type and amount of clothing the seamen should have. This included two blue jackets; six shirts, or four shirts and two frocks; two pairs of blue trousers and two pairs of white; two pairs of shoes; two pairs of stockings; two hats; one black silk handkerchief; and bedding. Some ships' 'slops' came ready-made but sometimes cloth was issued with needle and thread. The seamen were

expected to be uniformly dressed within a week, and expert sailors used to make the clothes of the inexpert in exchange for grog rations. The men made 'sennet' hats by weaving and shaping grass.

The year 1825 saw the first official illustrated dress regulations for naval officers. This ensured that the officers conformed to the wishes of the Lords Commissioners. The regulations were very explicit about the dress and accoutrement and went to considerable detail concerning hats, swords, breeches, shoe and knee buckles and all the other items that made up the naval officer's uniform. Flag officers removed the extra row of lace from the cuff, and the Admiral of the Fleet lost his special undress uniform. Lieutenants were ordered to wear a plain gold lace epaulette, without fringe, on the left shoulder, in addition to the fringed epaulette ordered in 1812. Officers of the various branches (Navigating, Medical, Secretarial and Accounting) were ordered a new full dress uniform consisting of a coat with lapels turned back and sewn down with plain button loops and nine buttons each side. There were three buttons on the cuff and the hip pockets as well as two each side of the skirt vent at the back.

The various ranks had embroidered devices on the collar. Masters of the Fleet and masters had the badge of the Navy Office; physicians and surgeons had the device of the defunct Sick and Hurt Office, which was an anchor with snake entwined; and pursers had the device of the Victualling Office. The first of the above pairs had the collar edged in gold lace. The secretary to the commander in chief had a crowned anchor on the collar, edged with gold lace, while secretaries to flag officers had the same device minus the gold lace edging. Master's mates were ordered a stand-up collar to their uniform with a gold lace button loop and button on the collar. The mate's single-breasted blue coat was edged in white around the front; collar, skirts, pocket flaps and cuffs were in white cloth. Midshipmen wore the same style of coat but with the white patch on the collar with button and white worsted

button loop. The new regulations also described the hats being bound in gold lace of varying widths depending on rank for all above lieutenant, that rank having black silk binding. Trousers both in blue and white cloth were now permitted in place of breeches and stockings, although there is no doubt that trousers had made their appearance *unofficially* at sea some decades previously.

A completely new undress uniform to be worn at sea was introduced consisting of a round jacket and round hat or cap. The round jacket was similar to the undress coat, i.e. blue cloth of similar cut to the full dress coat but devoid of lace, but without the skirts, at the rear. This was worn with the round black hat or a blue cap. The wearing of coats without tails was not new, as during the Napoleonic Wars, officers sometimes cut the tails from their coats for easier movement on board ship during active service. This practice presumably led to the tailless coat being 'regulated'.

In May 1827 it was decided that schoolmasters

6. **A lower deck of** *HMS Victory*, **showing arrangement of guns and equipment as well as the hanging tables and benches for the various 'messes'. (Commanding Officer** *HMS Victory* **[Ship])**

7. Full dress coat of Vice-Admiral Nelson, minus the epaulettes, which were gold with two silver stars on the straps. Note various embroidered orders on left breast. See colour plate B1. (National Maritime Museum)

should wear the same uniform as gunners, boat-swains and carpenters but without swords. The following month petty officers – who had no uniform – were ordered a device by which their rank could be recognized. First-class petty officers, including master-at-arms, were ordered a crowned anchor in white cloth to be worn on the left sleeve while second-class petty officers wore the anchor only.

The dress of the lower deck continued as before, with any uniformity that prevailed being due to the 'slop' issue and not to any regulations. However, in 1824, *Instructions for Pursers* ordered a long list of clothing which was to be kept on board ship. This included blue cloth jackets, knitted worsted waistcoats, blue cloth trousers, white trousers, frocks, shirts, stockings, hats and black silk hand-kerchiefs. In some ships, as in some regiments of the army, the captain supplied at his own expense certain items of dress to make his crew's appear-ance more uniform. At least one of these un-official additions at the expense of the captain gave the English language a new word and the Englishman a new garment. In the 1840s, the captain of *HMS Blazer* dressed his ship's company

in blue and white striped garment, which later in civilian wear took the name of that ship.

In 1827 a drastic alteration took place in the style and cut of the naval officer's coat. The new coat did not slope away from the waist to the rear but was cut around at the waist with the tails starting further towards the back, like a modern-day civilian evening dress tail-coat. The collar and cuffs were white edged in gold lace, the width varying with rank. The blue double-breasted coat was worn with blue trousers with a gold lace stripe down the seam in dress and with blue or white trousers in undress. Breeches were now reserved solely for the King's and Queen's draw-ing rooms. A short single-breasted great coat was introduced for wear by officers in the vicinity of their ships, but this garment akin, to the military frock coat, enjoyed a short life and was abolished in 1833. On this garment ranking was shown by gold lace bands on each cuff, but epaulettes were worn on the great coat by flag officers. Officers of the civil branches, warrant officers and those below the rank of Lieutenant retained their existing uniforms but were to wear them buttoned. This latter order seems not to have been strictly

8. *The Death of Nelson*, by D. Dighton. Many details of uniform, equipment, and fighting procedures can be picked out. Centre, in top hat, is Midshipman Pollock, who claimed to have killed the Frenchman who killed Nelson. (National Maritime Museum)

adhered to, as a number of contemporary prints show. Another major alteration was in the head dress. Warrant officers, Midshipmen, masters' assistants and volunteers, both first and second class lost their cocked hats and were ordered the round hat, all except warrant officers having it decorated with a loop of gold twisted wire. The following year, the blue great coat was ordered to be worn as undress and in 1829 a black leather waistbelt was introduced for wear with the coat.

Within a fortnight of the death of George IV, his brother William IV ordered that the face colours for naval officers should be scarlet and not white and that gold lace should not be worn on full dress trousers. Breeches were also finally abolished for drawing rooms. Naval officers did not have to wear trousers without lace for long;

flag officers had it restored in November 1830 and all other officers in October 1831.

In 1832, the shoulder belt worn under the waistcoat in full dress was finally abolished and a gold-embroidered waistbelt ordered in its place. Flag officers had the distinction of oak leaf embroidery with a line of gold embroidery top and bottom, captains and commanders had three lines of gold embroidery and lieutenants had two. In the same year, civil branch officers adopted the same uniform as the executive branch except that it was to be single-breasted with buttons in groups. The navigating branch had buttons at regular intervals: the medical branch in threes, the secretarial and accountants' branch in pairs. At the same time, the collar distinction of the various branches was abolished as were the various distinctive button designs.

In 1833, the greatcoat or morning coat was abolished and a return made to a double-breasted undress tail coat with buttons only for all beneath flag rank. Flag officers had their distinctive bands

9. 'Heaving the lead', a seaman of 1807; note loose frock over shirt, spotted scarf and straw hat. (National Maritime Museum)

of lace on the sleeve. Epaulettes were worn in undress but no strap was worn on the left shoulder by those officers so entitled in full dress. The civil branch undress, like their full dress coat, was single-breasted and the same distinction of button spacing was retained.

The Early Victorian Navy

The navy of the nineteenth century was a changing navy, even if many of the changes were slow. Steam power, which was to revolutionize the navy and its ships, was first introduced in 1822 when the *Comet* and the *Monkey* were used to tow sailing ships out of harbour when there was no wind. In 1826 the rating of stoker was introduced. In 1830 the first school of naval gunnery was opened at Portsmouth where selected seamen were sent for training. In 1831, as an inducement to long service, a pension scheme was introduced for those who served continuously for over twenty-one years. However, it was not until the middle of the reign of Queen Victoria that changes in propulsion and style of ships and their construction, guns and gunnery, propellents and projectiles, rates of pay and conditions, the introduction of uniforms for seamen and improvements in navigation and telegraphy laid the foundations of a modern and professional navy.

The opening years of the reign of Queen Victoria did not bring any startling changes in the dress of the navy. In November 1837, first engineers were ordered to wear the same uniform as carpenters, boatswains and gunners. In December 1841, however, first-class engineers were ordered a special uniform with their own buttons. This was a double-breasted blue coat with turned-down collar and round cuffs decorated with three buttons on each. The buttons, seven in number on each side, were grouped in fours. A single large button was worn on the collar. The buttons bore a steam engine with crown above, a sign of the navy's recognition of steam as a method of propulsion in the service, even if it was not popular. In December 1842, second and third-class engi-

10. Midshipman of 1823, a convincing coloured lithograph by C. Hullmaundel after F. W. Ommaney – except for the exaggerated shape of the trousers. (Parker Gallery)

neers adopted the same uniform, the distinction between classes being denoted by the size of the button on the collar. Second-class engineers used the standard coat button while third-class engineers used a waistcoat button. The distinctive uniform of engineers was abolished along with their special buttons in August 1853 when they were ordered the same uniform as the civil branches with eight buttons grouped in fours.

The most drastic change occurred in 1846, when the scarlet collar and cuffs introduced by William IV were discontinued and white collar and blue cuffs with white slashed flaps restored. At the same time, the lacing of skirts with gold lace stripes was reintroduced for officers of flag rank. In 1846, captains of less than three years adopted the crown for wear on the epaulettes in place of the anchor, which was given to commanders. Lieutenants were to wear a pair of plain epaulettes, while mates were to wear a single fringed epaulette on the right shoulder. Officers of flag rank adopted the crossed sword and baton insignia on the epaulette while an Admiral of the Fleet is described in the regulations of 1846 as having epaulettes with '. . . embroidered straps of acorn and oak leaf pattern with pearl crescent and edging. Three stars within the crescent and one on the strap; above it, crossed batons surmounted by a crown. A double row of dead and bright bullion three and a half inches long.' Officers of the Navigating branch were to wear the same uniform as the executive but with crossed anchors on the epaulette in place of the single foul anchor. Shoulder scales were permitted for wear in undress on board ship, but this was changed the following year when a double-breasted frock coat was introduced which displayed ranking on the cuff. For the first time, regulations ordered that a crown badge was to be worn on the cap above the band. Officers of *HMS Queen* seemed to have worn the crown badge some years before its official sanction.

The dress of the seaman had altered from that worn in the days of Nelson. Gone were the striped trousers and spotted handkerchiefs and in their place a more uniform dress was worn, though still regulated only by the supply of slops and not by any written orders or sealed patterns as in the

army. In the mid-1840s, the dress of the crew of the Royal Yacht *Victoria and Albert* was perhaps the most 'uniform' in the navy, and other captains attempted to copy this standard. The painting of H.R.H. Prince Edward Albert by Winterhalter shows the young prince in the summer rig of the Royal Yacht. It consisted of a white frock with blue cuffs, a broad blue collar edged with three white lines and white bell-bottomed trousers into which the frock was tucked. Beneath the frock a striped shirt with stand collar was worn, with a knotted black handkerchief. The ship's name and any mottoes space permitted were painted on the band around the sennet hat. Queen Victoria noted in her diary that the suit was '. . . beautifully made by a man on board who makes for our sailors'. A gesture by the authorities towards uniformity was made in 1845 when an issue of blue jean and Dutch tape was authorized for making '. . . blue collars, cuffs and facings' for duck frocks. No

11. *The Point of Honour*, **by Cruikshank, 1825: a seaman is about to be flogged on the deck of a man-o'-war when the true culprit confesses. (National Maritime Museum)**

12. Full-dress coat of a midshipman, 1827. This style continued in use until 1891, although details of cut changed with prevailing fashions. (National Maritime Museum)

Uniforms for Seamen

In 1856, following the report of a committee on uniforms, major alterations were made in the dress of officers which were implemented in a new edition of dress regulations in that year. However, the most important decision concerning dress was the implementing in January 1857 (circular letter 283, 30 January) of the report of the committee under Rear Admiral The Hon. Henry Rous on the desirability of introducing a uniform for seamen. Having ascertained the views of the commanders-in-chief at Portsmouth and Devonport, who in turn sounded out the officers under them, a complete uniform was issued to petty officers, seamen and boys. 'Uniform dress' was laid down as consisting of a blue cloth jacket and trousers; white duck trousers; a white frock; square blue collar on which were three rows of white tape; a pea jacket; a black silk scarf; a black canvas hat with a ribbon around the crown bearing the ship's name in gold letters; a working cap akin to that worn by officers but without the peak; and the sennet hat. Badges were blue on white uniforms and red on blue uniforms. To all seamen, men and boys newly joined, an issue of two hammocks, a mattress, a cover and a blanket was made. Those possessing items of uniform which conformed to the regulations were allowed money in lieu at the following scale:

Blue cloth jacket	17s. 8d.
Blue cloth trousers	11s. 7d.
Blue serge frock	8s. 6d.
White duck frock	2s. 9d.
White duck trousers	2s. 7d.
Black silk scarf	2s. 10d.
Pair of shoes	6s. 7d.

At the same time another commission improved the seaman's diet, and a third his terms of service, pay and rights to a pension after twenty-two years' service. Good conduct badges, gained after five years' good service and carrying an extra 3d. a day had been introduced in 1849. Special ships were set aside as training vessels for boys and junior seamen, and the facilities at the gunnery

mention was made concerning the number of white lines around the collar. When finally regulated to three, these lines had nothing to do with Nelson's victories, as legend supposes: the original recommendation was for two or four rows, and compromise made it three.

Various captains could still dress their crews as they wished, and the Sunday rig of the crew of *HMS Victory* was noted in 1850 as consisting of a '... short blue jacket with double rows of large mother of pearl buttons placed very close together, white frock with wide blue jean collar worn outside the jacket, and immensely wide blue cloth trousers.' Some captains were greater individualists. The captain of *HMS Caledonia* put his men in Scots bonnets, while another who had fought in the Greek War of Independence issued petticoat trousers to his crew, imitating the dress of Greek soldiers.

school *HMS Excellent* were enlarged to cope with the increased inflow of men wishing to be trained in their chosen profession.

The alteration in the dress of the officers brought about by the 1856 dress regulations involved some minor changes to the widths of lace on collar, cuff and pocket flaps. The denoting of rank by the use of laced stripes on the cuff was now ordered for all coats and not just the frock coat. For executive officers, the top stripe was to '. . . form a circle in the centre of the top sleeve'. This ambiguous description referred to the 'curl'. The civil branches, while having the ranking stripes omitted the 'curl'. The civil branches were further distinguished from the executive by having a gold anchor and crown as a cap badge in place of a silver

one introduced by the 1856 regulations for executive officers; gold lace rather than gold bullion loop to the cocked hat; and flat instead of round tassels to the hat. The epaulettes of the civil branches, instead of having the gold edging and silver wire devices of the executive, had silver edging and gold wire devices. The cap badge previously mentioned was in the form of a 'crown embroidered in gold and silver and a silver anchor, surrounded by laurel branches.' The regulations also ordered that the peak of the cap should be embroidered in gold for officers of the rank of commander and above. In 1860, gold

13. Master-at-arms or quartermaster, by Gauci, *c.*1828; a first class petty officer with crown and anchor badges on left arm. (Parker Gallery)

14. Captains, 1832; note scarlet collars and cuffs, button arrangement on skirts, sword belts and cocked hats. (Parker Gallery)

oak leaf embroidery was sanctioned for the peaks of caps of executive officers of the rank of commander and above, the plain embroidery being retained for officers of equal rank in the civil branches.

The single epaulette worn by mates, assistant surgeons, paymasters and assistant engineers first class was abolished, and a pair of scales without fringes was introduced with the edging in gold for executive and silver for civil branches.

In 1860, the badges worn by petty officers and seamen were ordered to be embroidered in red worsted for both white and blue clothing. The various badges in use at this time were:

Chief petty officer : Crown and anchor encircled with laurel (in 1879 laurel was replaced by oak leaves)
First-class petty officer : Crown and crossed anchors.
Second-class petty officer : Crown and anchor
Leading seaman : Anchor
Gunnery instructor : Gun, with rifle and cutlass crossed with crown above

Seaman gunner first class : Gun with crown above
Seaman gunner second class : Gun

As the century wore on and the navy became more technical, new weapons such as torpedoes were introduced and more and more specialist badges were sanctioned. In 1861, the mate became a commissioned officer and assumed the title of sub-lieutenant; in 1863 he was given a stripe of gold lace to the cuff instead of the braid previously worn by mates. Two years previously, officers of senior ranks had the number of stripes on the cuff altered. Lieutenants and masters of over eight years' service were given two stripes, Commanders added one to give three, and Captains added one to give them four. Commodores second class were ordered a single thick stripe of lace, three-quarters of an inch in width, with a 'curl' of half-inch wide lace above. In 1863 all Lieutenants and masters, whatever their seniority, assumed the two stripes.

In the same year, coloured velvet placed between the lace stripes was introduced to indicate the civil branch of the wearer. These were:

Navigating Branch : light blue (abolished 1867)
Medical Branch : scarlet
Accountant Branch : white
Engineers : purple

Another innovation of that year was the sanctioning of a white linen cap cover to be worn by all ranks in hot weather. The order did not, however, appear to be explicit enough and various forms of cover appeared. Some officers covered the crown; some the entire cap including the peak; while others adopted this latter style but left a neat cut-out for the cap badge to show through.

In 1865 the ranks of chief gunner, chief boatswain and chief carpenter were introduced and were denoted by a half-inch stripe of lace on the cuff. In the same year officers were ordered not to wear white trousers with full dress. In 1868 the old style cap ribbon, on which the name of the ship was painted, was at last replaced by a ribbon with the ship's name in gilt wire. Some captains, at their own expense, had had the cap ribbons embroidered instead of painted. The following year the Admiralty announced that, 'Representations having been made to their Lordships that it would conduce to the health and comfort of men under many circumstances of service, were they permitted to discontinue the use of the Razor on board her Majesty's ships'; those who so wished could wear beards and moustaches. However, the instructions stated that the beard and moustache had to be worn together. Furthermore, those with the 'full set' were to keep it in neat trimmed order and the captains of ships were to see that the hair on the head and face was to be kept to the same length.

Birth of the Modern Navy

One of the greatest leaps forward in the history of the Royal Navy took place on 3 December 1860 when the first iron-hulled, armoured frigate – *HMS Warrior* – was launched. She carried twenty-eight 68 pdr muzzle-loading guns, ten 110 pdr breech-loading Armstrong guns and four 70 pdr breech-loading Armstrong guns. She had a speed of ten knots under steam and fourteen with sail and carried armour plate four-and-a-half inches thick backed by eighteen inches of teak. There were other signs that the navy was rapidly modernizing. In 1860 the last man (a Marine) was hanged at the yard-arm, and although flogging was not suspended in peace and war until 1879, it was quickly becoming a thing of the past. The old Articles of War which had governed naval discipline for hundreds of years were replaced in 1861 by the Naval Discipline Act, which in turn was superseded by a new Naval Discipline Act in 1866. In 1866 the savings banks which had existed for some years in the army were established for seamen and marines. The 1860s marked the end of the old navy and the birth of the new.

Despite the appearance of dress regulations for officers and the issue of uniform clothing for seamen there was still a noticeable degree of individuality among both officers and men during the 1860s and 1870s. Once again, differences between

ships were noticed and a number of high-ranking officers voiced their complaints to the Admiralty. Admiral George Elliot wrote in 1875 that he had noticed such strange attire as overcoats, mackintoshes and cloaks and capes of differing cut and colour, and he also saw some officers actually carrying umbrellas! The Admiral also remarked on the differing styles of neckwear of both officers and seamen. Other letters from various stations began to arrive at the Admiralty. From the Pacific station, complaints were made about the length of the skirts of the frock coats, some being comically long while others were so short as to be '. . . a kind of German tunic'. Some officers wore the coat buttoned; others left it open. Having recorded their disgust at the non-uniformity of the officers, the various writers turned their attention to the lower deck. 'Can it be wondered that the men break out into little bits of silk embroidery of different colours and adorn the borders of their black silk handkerchiefs . . . that their blue jean collars are occasionally too large, the tape not quite regulations and their caps of peculiar shape?'

In 1879 certain irregularities in the cut and style of officers' uniforms were remedied by the publication of illustrated dress regulations, but even this did not stifle individuality altogether. For example, since 1825 the regulation neckwear had

15. **Volunteers of the First Class and volunteer of the Second Class, *c.*1834. Note dirks, round hats, and button loop on collar. (Parker Gallery)**

been a black silk cravat or stock, but all officers preferred a conventional tie or in some cases a bow tie. The irregularities in the shirts worn by other ranks, 'white, coloured, flannel with paper collars and false fronts' continued until the introduction of the white flannel shirt bound at the neck with blue tape. In 1880 two new garments were added to the issue for seamen. These were the blue serge and white duck jumpers which were worn outside the trousers and incorporated a knife pocket on the left breast, the lanyard being worn around the neck. On frocks and jumpers used for ceremonial, watch stripes were worn. These, red on blue clothing and blue on white, were stripes sewn where the sleeve joined the shoulder. A stripe on the right arm denoted starboard watch and on the left arm, port watch.

The beginning of the 1880s once more saw the navy engaged on land with the army. They had previously been engaged in various campaigns including the Indian Mutiny of 1857, the China War of 1860, the Abyssinia campaign of 1868, the Ashanti War of 1874 and the Zulu War of 1879. In the Mutiny, sailors forming *HMS Shannon*'s naval brigade wore white duck trousers with blue frocks tucked into them. The usual head dress was the round hat with white cover. Captain William Peel wore a white wicker helmet covered in cloth and wound around with a *paggri* which hung down behind as a neck flap. He wore, according to contemporary prints, a white shirt with butterfly collar and black tie, white waistcoat and white trousers. Over this he

16. Captain, flag officer and commander in undress, 1829–33. The officers wear the 1827 undress coat with the 1829 swordbelt. Note ranking on cuff of Captain (left) and Commander (right) and the Admiral's epaulettes. (Parker Gallery)

wore a blue frock coat with gold lace ranking on the cuff. The strangest part of his equipment was a copy of a Roman legionary's sword carried in a steel scabbard with brass mounts! Other officers wore round hats with white covers. In the Abyssinian campaign, the naval brigade formed from the crews of various ships wore blue frocks and trousers, brown leather equipment and sennet hats. They had charge of the rocket tubes which decimated the forces of King Theodore. In the Ashanti War of 1874 the naval brigade, 400 strong, was landed from a number of ships. The uniform worn by seamen of the naval brigade was described by H. M. Stanley, the war correspondent of the *New York Herald* as being '. . . the naval blue shirt and wide trousers, which they use on board, while they appeared somewhat jauntier in their broad-brimmed straw hats, covered with a canvas cape fastened around the hat by a brown muslin veil'.

During the Zulu War of 1879, the naval brigade was once more engaged. They wore the usual blue frock and trousers, brown leather equipment, and the sennet hat, sailors' cap, or the foreign service helmet issued to the army. A white helmet was not authorized for naval officers and men until 1881. Photographs of the naval brigade in the Zulu and First Boer Wars show the officers wearing blue helmets, sometimes with a brass spike on the top, and the men wearing the round seaman's hat with the white cover stained.

In the war against the Egyptians under Arabi Pasha in 1881–2, the 'blue jackets' landed in Alexandria wore white trousers, sennet hats and blue jackets. During this war the commander-in-chief, Mediterranean, was given authority to make modifications to uniforms when conditions demanded. Consequently there were various combinations of white and blue or all-white, and the adoption of the white military helmet. During the later campaigns against the Dervishes, involving the relief of Khartoum, the sailors wore blue frocks and trousers, brown leather equipment, and sennet hats or sailors' caps. The sennet hats assumed extraordinary shapes, either intended by the wearer or because of campaign conditions. Other ranks usually wore the haversack, which was intended to be worn on a strap across the body and hanging from the left hip, on the back,

17. H.R.H. Prince Albert Edward (later Edward VII) in uniform of the Royal Yacht *Victoria and Albert*, made for him by a member of the crew. Note 'watch stripes' on upper arms. By F. Winterhalter, *c*.1846. (By gracious permission of HM The Queen)

with the water bottle clipped to the waistbelt beneath it. The illustration of Captain Wilson, RN, winning the Victoria Cross at the battle of El Teb shows him wearing the white helmet, a blue single-breasted jacket with ranking in gold lace on the cuff, blue trousers tucked into leggings, and black leather undress sword belt with holster. Haversack and water bottle were also carried.

While discipline was still severe, it was not as oppressive as it had been in the past. Two important punishments were withdrawn in the late Victorian era. In 1871, the Admiralty directed that corporal punishment should be restricted in peacetime; and in 1879 flogging was *suspended* in peace and war – it was *not* abolished! An unexplained mystery is that the last flogging that took place on board ship, with mustered ship's company, was in 1880. Finally, in 1939, the 'cat-o'-nine tails' was abolished.

It was not until 1885 that an established tropical uniform for officers, consisting of white helmet with blue *paggri*, white tunic and trousers was authorized. Ranking was denoted by stripes in white silk on the cuff. At the same time a blue tunic was introduced to replace the ship jacket. It was abandoned in 1889 when the 'monkey jacket' replaced it. Two years later a monkey jacket was introduced for seamen, to replace the round jacket. It was intended to be worn on duty or on leave, in cold and wet weather. The blue jean collar was worn on the outside except in rainy weather.

In 1891 a further edition of dress regulations was published. This was the third illustrated version to appear and detailed in words and illustrations the eight 'dresses' authorized for naval officers. These 'dresses' were as follows:

No. 1: Full dress
No. 2: Ball dress
No. 3: Frock coat with epaulettes
No. 4: Frock coat
No. 5: Undress coat
No. 6: Mess dress
No. 7: Mess undress
No. 8: White undress

The principal changes in the new regulations were that the number of buttons on the full dress coat was reduced from ten each side to eight, and the gold lace that adorned the skirts of Flag Officers' coats was dispensed with. The undress coat, with slight modifications, was to constitute the ball dress worn with wing collar, stiff-fronted

18. Admiral (right), captain (centre) and commodore (left) with midshipman and marine in background, 1846–56. Note the Mameluke sword worn by flag officers 1842–56; although it was abolished in the latter year, Admiral of the Fleet Sir Henry Keppel, G.C.B. – who did not reach flag rank until 1857 – is seen wearing this non-regulation weapon in a photo as late as 1896. (Parker Gallery)

19. Captain, lieutenant and seaman, 1846–56, with marine in background. Note 'uniform' appearance of seaman, although his costume was not covered by regulations at this date. This type of rig was to be the forerunner of naval dress the world over. (Parker Gallery)

shirt and waistcoat. The frock coat was modified in cut and by the removal of the buttons from the cuff, except for warrant officers, and the monkey jacket was approved for normal undress wear on most occasions. The new uniform introduced the blue and white mess jackets with blue and white waistcoats, the blue pattern being edged in gold braid. In 1903 the gold braid disappeared from the mess waistcoat. The round jacket was abolished for all except midshipmen and cadets, with a reduction in the number of buttons from nine to seven. On greatcoats and white tunics shoulder straps to show rank were introduced, and the epaulettes of Admiral of the Fleet now displayed a badge of the crown above crossed batons surrounded by laurel leaves. For the civil branches, the greatest change was the abolition of button grouping distinctions to show the branch, and adoption of the double-breasted coat. The regulations also introduced the boat cloak and gaiters for officers. The gaiters were of patent leather of the same design as worn by petty officers and seamen.

20. Seamen, 1854; from left to right: Charles Brooks, Admiral's Coxswain, *HMS Britannia*; John Stanley, Boatswain, *HMS Sampson*; and Edward Penelly, leading seaman, *HMS Sans Pareil*. Note heavily buttoned jackets, tarred hat, and collar worn over the coat by Penelly. (Wilkinson-Latham Collection)

The dress of seamen was also regulated further by the establishment of orders of dress. They also numbered eight and were as follows:

No. 1: Blue serge frock with gilt embroidered badges, collar and cloth trousers
No. 2: As above but badges in red worsted embroidery
No. 3: Serge jumper, collar and trousers
No. 4: As above but without collar
No. 5: White working jumper, duck trousers, check shirt
No. 6: White drill frock and trousers
No. 7: Duck jumper, collar and trousers
No. 8: Serge jumper, collar and duck trousers

Despite the strict orders of dress, certain irregularities were overlooked and sometimes even encouraged. One such occasion was the

21. Sir William Peel, as a captain R.N. during the Indian Mutiny. Note wicker helmet with cloth cover, frock coat, and 'Bluejackets' in background with frocks and sennet hats. Peel holds the regulation sword here; in fact he carried a privately ordered replica of a Roman *gladius* made by Henry Wilkinson. (National Maritime Museum)

On 11 October 1899 war broke out between the British and the Boers in South Africa, and for those officers and men who formed the naval brigade it meant a radical change in uniform. No longer was the blue or white suitable and the seamen, warrant officers and officers were ordered to be dressed in khaki. Officers wore the military helmet with khaki cover, the military tunic with naval buttons and ranking in gold lace on blue shoulder boards, khaki breeches and dark blue puttees. The equipment – consisting of waistbelt, braces, holster and ammunition pouch – was of the same pattern as issued to seamen (who did not, of course, wear the revolver holster and pouch but two ammunition pouches). Some officers preferred to wear the army officer's Sam Browne belt, holster, pouch, braces and sword frog. The sword carried in the frog usually had a canvas cover to the scabbard to hide the brass mounts. Seamen wore the same khaki uniform as issued to other ranks in the army but exchanged the helmet for the sennet hat with khaki cover, placing the band with the ship's name over the cover. Canvas leggings replaced the military puttees. The equipment comprised a brown leather waistbelt and two divided braces. For chief petty officers this equipment was worn with revolver holster and ammunition pouch but the seamen had two ammunition pouches on the front, a haversack and waterbottle, an additional 'expense' pouch at the back and a bandolier-type arrangement across the body holding additional rounds of ammunition. In 1901, the naval brigade returned to their ships and their traditional uniform.

Even while the war raged, their Lordships continued to tinker with naval dress. In December 1900, oak leaf embroidery was introduced for the collar and around the cuff beneath the ranking lace on the full dress coat of flag officers. The broad band of lace previously used was abandoned. The following year, the full dress coat of flag officers was again modified by the addition of a band of gold piping above the embroidery on the cuff and by placing the lace stripes above it and not centred on the slashed flap. In 1904, the flag officer's coat was modified again by the removal of the embroidery on the cuff and the substitution of a broad lace stripe. The laced white slashed flap was replaced by a white one

Queen's Jubilee in 1887, when the crew of the *Egeria* were given permission to wear any clothing they wished. A seaman on board recorded that 'there were some very curious rigs amongst them'. A first-class petty officer dressed as a seaman is shown in Fig. 29 wearing No. 1 dress. Ratings (and there were quite a number, such as ships' corporals, sick berth attendants, waiters and cooks) wore a single- or double-breasted version of the chief petty officer's coat, but with black buttons showing crown and anchor, and a peaked cap with badge in red worsted embroidery. This was known as 'fore and aft rig'.

Just prior to the outbreak of the Boer War in 1899, it was decreed that miniature medals would be worn with ball dress instead of full size campaign medals and decorations, when the wearer found the number he had won or had been awarded were an 'inconveniencey'.

embroidered with oak leaf design.

In 1906 the shape of the white helmet was altered to the new Wolseley pattern, but the most significant change was in the dress of seamen. Frocks were abolished and their place was taken by blue serge jumpers with buttons fastening the cuff. As early as 1880 frocks which were designed to be tucked in the trousers were permitted to be worn outside. Frocks tucked into trousers, however, were still worn by the crew of the Royal Yacht by the express order of Edward VII. They also had the added distinction of silver rather than gold embroidered badges.

Two jumpers were issued to seamen, the No. 1 with buttoned cuffs and gold embroidered badges and the No. 2 without buttoned cuffs and with the badges in red worsted on blue cloth. When the No. 1 jumper became worn, the cuffs and badges were removed and it became a No. 2 with red worsted badges added. Other new garments were the combination blue jean suit and the canvas overall, which were used for such work as coaling and general maintenance work aboard ship. In 1910 the trousers of seamen were given the uniform width at the bottom of twelve inches.

In 1904 an event of enormous significance for the Royal Navy took place – the appointment of Admiral Sir John Fisher as First Sea Lord.

'Jacky' Fisher was a visionary individualist who feared no man – or committee – on earth. His plans for dragging the navy kicking and screaming into the twentieth century had been formulated before he became First Sea Lord; now he rushed them into effect. He believed that a ruthless rationalization programme was necessary, based on only four classes of warships: battleships, armoured cruisers, destroyers and submarines. Across a list of 154 vessels he scrawled the brief comment, 'Scrap the lot!' The great Victorian boast that the Royal Navy was the largest in the world concealed much muddle and lack of co-ordination. In 1897 there were 387 vessels in the fleet, both in and out of commission, but many were obsolete, and the total represented eighteen types of ship. By September 1914 there were 638 of only ten types, including 334 destroyers and torpedo boats, and 65 battleships of which 25 were 'dreadnoughts'. These latter, named after *HMS Dreadnought*, whose keel was laid in 1906, were Fisher's pride. The first ship in the class was two years ahead of the world, a metal-clad monster of 17,900 tons capable of 21 knots and armed with a great battery of 12-in guns.

'Jacky' did not confine himself to the building

22. A crowded print illustrating all ranks of the Royal Navy, Royal Marine Artillery and Royal Marines in 1869. (Parker Gallery)

23. Officers of *HMS Active* near the lower Tugela River during the Zulu War, 1879. Note leggings, revolver crossbelts, and ammunition pouches. (National Army Museum)

programme. He revised training methods, building proper shore establishments and scrapping the old 'hulks'; he established Dartmouth and Osborne naval colleges; he improved pay and conditions, and raised standards of professionalism. He looked into the most obscure corners himself, and in the field of individual armament his attitude was typical: he ordered the withdrawal and sale from the stores of the age-old 'boarding pike', remarking that while he was about it he had had a good look around to see if there were any bows and arrows still on the inventory! (It is worth noting that the fearful cutlass, the boarder's other traditional weapon, was to remain in use until 1936.)

In 1911 officers were permitted to wear shirts with soft fronts and stiff collars; and the following year the rank of mate was re-introduced for promotion from the lower deck. An omen of the future was the ordering of gilt 'wings' to be worn on the left breast in 1913 by naval pilots; and the formation the following year of the Royal Naval Air Service, whose distinctive eagle badge was worn in place of the anchor on buttons, cap badges, sword belts, swords and epaulettes.

The World Wars

It took until January 1916 for the Admiralty to announce that full dress, ball dress, frock coats and mess dress were to be abolished for the duration of the war. Some time previously they had ordered that engineer officers would wear the same uniform as executive officers and that the braid forming the stripes of the Royal Naval Reserve and the Royal Naval Volunteer Reserve should be replaced by quarter-inch gold lace. In 1916 there were a number of other changes in dress for officers. In January permission was given for soft collars to be worn at sea, and grey trousers and soft collars could be worn with the monkey jacket when on shore 'for recreation'. In May, a blue beaver watch coat similar to the army's 'British warm' was made an alternative to the greatcoat. In August wound stripes were introduced, consisting of two inches of Russia braid. One of these stripes was sewn to the left sleeve for every wound suffered. In October khaki uniforms were sanctioned for officers employed ashore outside

1 Midshipman, 1795
2 Master and Commander, 1790
3 Cabin boy, 1800

G. A. EMBLETON

A

1 Vice-Admiral Lord Nelson,
  Trafalgar, 1805
2 Surgeon, 1805
3 Seaman, 1805

B

G. A. EMBLETON

1 Commander, 1830
2 Boatswain, 1828
3 Seaman, 1828

G. A. EMBLETON

C

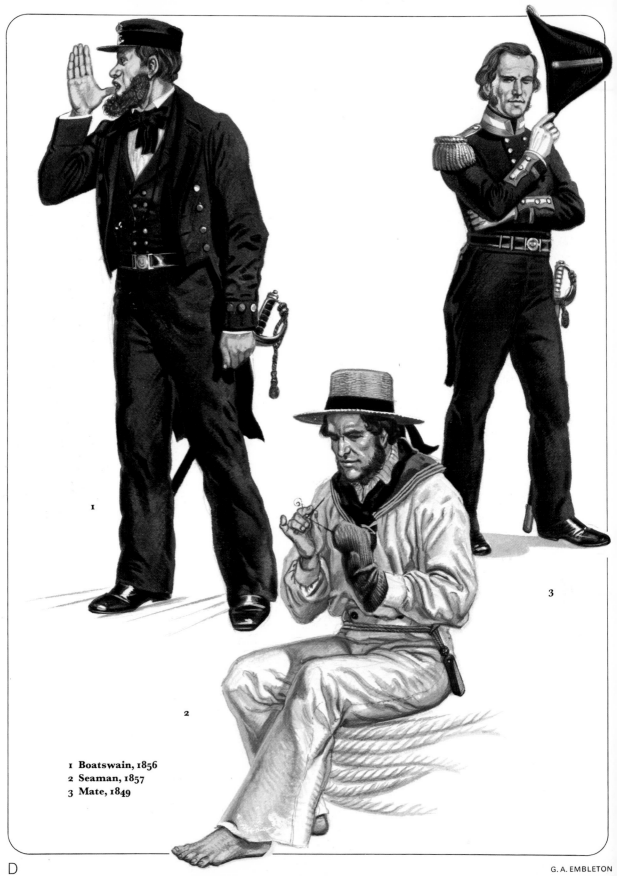

1 Boatswain, 1856
2 Seaman, 1857
3 Mate, 1849

D

G. A. EMBLETON

1 Lieutenant, Royal Naval Reserve, 1864
2 Seaman, Naval Brigade, 1882
3 Assistant Surgeon, 1860

G. A. EMBLETON

E

1 Captain, 1900
2 Lieutenant, Engineering Branch, 1902
3 Petty Officer, 1899

F

G. A. EMBLETON

G. A. EMBLETON

1 Seaman, 1925
2 Lieutenant, 1942
3 Leading Patrolman, 1949

G

H

1 **Lieutenant-Commander, 1970**
2 **Seaman, 1970**
3 **Lieutenant, Fleet Air Arm, 1970**

G. A. EMBLETON

Britain. The tunics were the same as those worn by army officers with the ranking stripes in khaki braid on the cuffs. Brass naval buttons were worn but these were later changed to bronze. The naval cap was worn with a khaki cap cover but permission was given for a khaki cap with bronze badge to be worn 'when exposed to enemy fire'. Trousers were also khaki and breeches were in Bedford cord. With this uniform the Sam Browne was used, and the shoes were to be brown with plain toe caps. There also existed a khaki drill version of the uniform which was worn with the foreign service helmet covered in khaki drill in hot climates 'when exposed to enemy fire'.

In October 1918 executive titles were given to all officers, the difference between the executive and civil branches abolished, and the 'curl' in the top lace cuff stripe extended to all. The only distinction now was the coloured cloth. Warrant officers were ordered to wear commissioned officers' swords and to have a quarter-inch stripe on the cuff in place of the three buttons. They were also ordered the same full dress coat as commissioned officers but with narrower lace. The Wardmaster branch replaced its scarlet cloth distinction with maroon, while new colours were introduced for shipwright officers (silver-grey), electrical officers (dark green), and ordnance officers (dark blue). Dental officers were given orange cloth in the 1920s.

It is interesting to note that after the First World War 'prize money', a perk of the navy since time immemorial, was paid. A slight difference from the days was that the money was not alloted to any individual ship as a result of capture but to all serving at sea. In 1919, it was calculated that the 'prize money' available for distribution amounted to £14,000,000. Admiral Beatty and others of his rank received £4,000, the amount descending through the ranks to the able seamen, who received £25.

After the war the Admiralty set about again 'improving' or altering the design of clothing, but introduced little of consequence except the restriction of full dress, a costly item, to *levées* at home. On all other occasions, the frock coat with epaulettes was ordered. In 1928 soft-fronted shirts were permitted with mess dress and shirts with soft cuffs were allowed with the monkey jacket. In July 1930 officers of the rank of commander and above were required to provide themselves with full dress, and in 1938 tropical dress of white shirt with shoulder straps (without tie), white shorts and white or blue socks was introduced. Either the cap or the helmet could be worn with this rig. A redesigned frock coat

24. Naval Brigade in South Africa, 1879–80. Note blue covers on officers' helmets, seaman's covered cap. The weapon is the Gatling machine-gun, traditionally served by naval crews in colonial campaigns. (National Army Museum)

25. 'Bluejackets' (left, behind gibbet) watching hanging of a
looter in Alexandria, 1882. The short blue jackets and sennet
hats are just visible. (Isabel and Aline Scott-Elliot)

was introduced in 1933 with only four buttons each side, three of which were buttoned. This enabled longer lapels to be incorporated, keeping up with the civilian fashions.

In 1934 the traditional black silk handkerchief was altered from square to oblong. It was now no longer necessary to carefully roll the square and tie it at the back; the seamen had only to loop it, and sew the ends together at the convenient place so that it could be slipped on and off over the head. The loose ends on the chest were fastened by loops through the jumper which were tied in a bow over the handkerchief. In 1938 the white flannel shirt was changed to cotton but still retained the distinctive square neck bound in blue tape.

In 1940, white cap covers were discontinued in home waters for the duration. The following year khaki battledress was approved for officers in beach parties, but blue battledress was strictly forbidden until 1943, when a working dress on those lines was approved. In 1941, as an economy measure, ranking stripes were to go only half way around the cuff. In 1944 more cuts in cost were ordered. Woven lace was used for ranking on shoulder straps in place of woven wire lace, and an all-metal cap badge was introduced. In May 1945 a khaki tropical dress was authorized of bush shirt, khaki drill shorts, cap with khaki cover, khaki stockings and brown or black shoes. In April 1946 white cap covers were reintroduced, and in May it was ordered that bow ties should be worn with the monkey jacket pending the reintroduction of mess dress.

Today's Navy

In December 1945, the First Lord of the Admiralty announced that prize money would be paid for the last time. The amount available for distribution was only £5,250,000, and of this £1,250,000 was handed over to the Royal Air Force for their part in operations at sea. The monies received by officers, seamen and marines ranged from £60 for a senior flag officer to £6 for a seaman.

In 1947 the full round lace stripes were restored to the sleeve; in 1949 the wearing of full dress was

26. Captain A. Wilson at the battle of El Teb, showing the uniform worn by officers in the Sudan. Note the flop-brim sennet hats and equipment of seamen in background. Wilson, whose sword broke between the ribs of a Dervish, was awarded the Victoria Cross for his courage in saving the life of one of his men by fighting off the Dervishes with his fists and the broken hilt of his weapon. (Wilkinson-Latham Collection)

placed in abeyance, and frock coats and white helmet were abolished. A modified form of mess dress was introduced. Later that year, the ceremonial uniform was ordered to be the monkey jacket (or white tunic) with decorations, medals and swords. The modifications carried out since that date include the disappearance of the Royal Naval Reserve and Royal Naval Volunteer Reserve rank waves on the sleeves and the substitution of the normal stripe with the letter 'R' in the 'curl', this to be omitted on mobilization. In 1955 the coloured cloth distinctions were removed from cuffs, except for medical, dental and wardmaster officers. The following year blue caps were abolished and the white-topped cap was worn all the year round. In 1959 a ceremonial coat with six buttons was introduced for flag officers, to be worn with the peaked cap, full-dress sword belt, and shoulder boards in place of epaulettes. In 1960 admirals of the fleet were further distinguished by having eight buttons on the ceremonial coat and the sword belt with oak leaf embroidery was reinstated.

Soon afterwards a complete list of revised rigs was issued. This consisted of nineteen possibilities, five more than pre-war, but simplified and more in keeping with modern conditions. They included special working dress, tropical dress and active service dress.

After the war, the pre-war overalls of seamen were replaced by a more sensible working rig of a light blue shirt and dark blue denim trousers. At the same time a white plastic-topped cap was issued for wear all year round. New white uniforms were introduced for tropical and special working dresses for specialized occasions. In 1956 junior ratings of the Supply, Secretarial, Sick Berth and Code Branches, who had worn

Class III rig of 'fore-and-aft' jackets with black buttons, straight trousers and peaked cap with red embroidered badge, were ordered to wear 'square rig' with bell-bottomed trousers, jumper and collar. The duffel coat was replaced after seventy years' service with specially-designed garments lined against the cold with kapok, to be worn under waterproofed clothing. Oilskins were replaced by PVC impregnated cloth and raincoats were given detachable linings for warmth. Seamen were issued with sheets and pyjamas in ships as well as on shore and the hammock gave way to tubular steel and canvas bunks. In 1956 a blue jean collar combined with waistcoat was introduced, as was a new pattern zip-fronted jumper of smooth serge. The old style naval leggings gradually gave way to the standard 'gaiter', similar to that worn by the army. In 1958 an arm badge was designed for submarine ratings but it was not issued. In 1971 a gilt metal brooch was approved to be worn on the chest above medal ribbons. In 1957 the traditional naval custom of junior ratings removing their

27. Officers of _HMS Terrible_ in the late 1890s. (Wilkinson-Latham Collection)

caps at the paymaster's desk so that their money could be tipped on top was abolished. While this might have been suitable when the seaman's pay consisted of a few coins, his modern pay in notes made this practice outdated.

On 31 July 1970, the Admiralty announced that '... in the light of the conditions of the modern Navy the rum issue is no longer compatible with the high standard of efficiency required now that the individual's tasks in ships are concerned with complex and often delicate machinery and systems, on the correct functioning of which peoples' lives may depend'. But, as with the uniform dress of the Royal Navy, traditions die hard, and rum is still made available for special occasions, when the signal 'Splice the Mainbrace' is made.

28. Sailors and marines (in fatigue caps) line up for their meat rations, carefully weighed under the eagle eye of a chief petty officer. (Wilkinson-Latham Collection)

The Plates

A1 Midshipman, 1795

The dress shown here was described in the 1787 regulations as: 'Blue Cloth Coat, no Lapels, Blue round Cuff, with Three Buttons, and Three to the Pocket; stand-up Collar, with small White turnback as before; White Lining but not edged; Buttons same as Warrant Officers; White Cloth Waistcoat and Breeches.' The cocked hat illustrated was sometimes replaced by a high, round hat resembling a civilian top hat. The stock was either white or black and usually a shirt frill showed above the waistcoat. The black cross-belt fastened with an oval gilt plate, and from it

29. First Class petty officer dressed – perhaps unusually – in 'square rig', c.1896. (National Maritime Museum)

was suspended an ivory-hilted dirk. Dirks were of various patterns, being governed by no regulation. Many details of the uniforms of these young men – who often went to sea on active service at twelve years old – were a reflection of their fathers' income.

A2 Master and Commander, 1790
The November 1787 regulations describe the full dress as: 'Blue Cloth Coats, with Blue Lapels, round Cuffs, laced with Gold Lace; the Pocket once laced, and one on the Cuff; Three Buttons to each; stand-up Collar double-laced; White Lining; Buttons as above; White Cloth Waistcoat and Breeches, plain.' Head dress was not mentioned and was left very much to individuals; the full dress hat was edged with gold lace and the 'plain' hat with black braid. The method of wear was also at personal discretion. The straight

sword was worn suspended from a black crossbelt, and had a gilt and ivory hilt; the belt was fastened by a gilt oval plate engraved with an anchor or the ship's name, and other designs at the owner's discretion.

A3 Ship's boy, 1800
This plate is taken from Rowlandson's well-known set of prints. The black tarred hat is typical of seamen of the day, as are the coloured scarf, shirt and waistcoat. Trousers of white or striped cloth were worn, or the canvas 'petticoat' trousers shown here, which gave easy movement and protection from the wet when at boat work or manning the yards. White stockings and plain square-toed black shoes completed the normal dress. The blue jacket was almost universal, and the men often decorated them with buttons at their own expense. The cost of the 'slops', issued by the purser after ordering a bulk quantity from victualling yards, was deducted from the men's pay, a system providing the often-venal purser with many opportunities for speculation.

B1 Vice-Admiral Lord Nelson, Trafalgar, 1805
The undress uniform worn at the Battle of Trafalgar, decorated only with two broad lace bands and buttons at the cuff. The hat bears two personal touches: instead of the usual black cockade it is distinguished by the diamond and silver *chelengk* ornament presented to Nelson after his victory at Aboukir by the Sultan of Turkey; and it has a green eyeshade fastened to the headband, folding down when required. On the breast are sewn bullion representations of the stars of his various orders: the Sicilian Order of St. Ferdinand and of Merit; the Order of the Bath; the Turkish Order of the Crescent; and the Equestrian Order of St. Joachim of Leiningen. The ribbons of these orders were worn over the waistcoat, only partly visible. At the throat he wears his two gold medals for St. Vincent and the Nile, on white ribbon edged blue (concealed from this angle by the lace frill but visible from the side). Also obscured here are the two silver stars on each epaulette strap. Note the absence of the sword – Nelson left it lying on his cabin table throughout the battle.

30. **Diver in full working rig, with handlers, at about the turn of the century. (Wilkinson-Latham Collection)**

31. Pay parade: a First Class petty officer in tropical whites receives his pay and places it on top of his cap, a tradition in the Royal Navy until recent times. (Wilkinson-Latham Collection)

B2 Surgeon, 1805

A circular letter of June 1805 first ordered a uniform dress for medical officers; the full dress, as shown, was to be the same as that of Physicians but without gold lace or epaulettes, rank being denoted by a loop of chain-pattern lace on the collar. Surgeons were unhappy at the lack of epaulettes, which were worn by their Army opposite numbers, and petitioned that they would be '. . . daily liable to meet with Army Medical Officers' and would be placed at a social disadvantage.

B3 Seaman, 1805

For general comments see A3. There were no regulations, and details were governed by the taste and pocket of the captain and the honesty of the purser, although certain general fashions emerged. The tarred hat and short blue jacket, decorated by the men with tape and buttons, are typical, as is the black silk scarf. In action this was tied round the head to protect the eyes from sweat and the ears from the cuncussion of the guns. Seamen vied in growing long, greased pigtails as a mark of long service. It is thought that tattoos were first applied by European seamen following the encounter between Captain James Cook's crew and tattooed islanders of King George's Island on Cook's first voyage of discovery. The fad spread quickly among sea-faring men.

C1 Commander, 1830

10 July 1830 saw the white collars and cuffs of naval officers' uniforms replaced by red at the whim of King William IV; gold-laced trousers and breeches were also briefly abolished, for a year only. In 1827 it had been ordered that the

uniform should consist of a single double-breasted coat, always to be worn buttoned. 1828 saw the introduction of a single-breasted greatcoat similar to the military frock coat.

C2 Boatswain, 1828

The uniform adopted in 1825 with the round hat adopted in 1827 for warrant officers not ranking with commissioned officers. It was worn until replaced by the peaked cap in 1856. This blue tail coat has two rows of buttons down the front, three on each cuff, three on the rear tail below the pocket flap, and two lower down on the tails. The 1805 pattern sword is suspended on the left from a black waist belt; although officially superseded by a new pattern in 1827, the old model continued to be widely used.

C3 Seaman, 1828

This formidable tar, on shore leave from *HMS Euryalus*, still wears an outfit typical of the Georgian period: white canvas blouse and trousers provided by the 'slop chest', with a personally purchased and decorated jacket and scarf, and a

32. **Lieutenant in ball dress, from the illustrated uniform regulations of 1891. This uniform has survived virtually unaltered. (National Maritime Museum)**

33. **Full-dress uniform of an admiral, 1904. Note embroidered collar and slashed cuff flaps, and embroidered flag officers' swordbelt. (National Maritime Museum)**

34. Anti-aircraft gun crew on a First World War battleship display blue, white and working uniforms. (Wilkinson-Latham Collection)

tarred hat decorated with painted motifs. These usually figured the name of the ship, or some loyal slogan. The pigtail had generally disappeared by about 1820. The gaudy hose worn by this seagoing hard-case are the sort of ridiculous affectation beloved of sailors of the period. His female companion wears costume typical of the more flamboyant working girls of Portsmouth Point.

D1 Boatswain, 1856

The 1856 peaked cap is illustrated, with black band, small black peak, and embroidered badge of a crown in heraldic colours above a silver foul anchor. The uniform is basically unchanged from the 1830s although the 1827 sword is now worn. The commissioned officers' sword was ordered for warrant officers only in 1918, after which date the black-gripped type was retained by the Master-at-Arms alone. Note the silver 'bo'sun's call' carried in the vest pocket on a black cord round the neck.

35. Seamen watching surrender of German High Seas Fleet at Scapa Flow, 1918. Note shape of blue caps. (Wilkinson-Latham Collection)

36. Bluejackets and marines at Archangel, Russia, during the Allied intervention of 1919. Note equipment of parading seamen. (Wilkinson-Latham Collection)

D2 Seaman, 1857

Bulk buying brought a certain standardization to the dress of the fo'c'sle by the middle of the century; but it was not until 1856 that a committee sat to report on the desirability of adopting a regulation uniform. A uniform for petty officers, seamen and boys was ordered in January 1857; illustrated here is the hot-weather version, a white frock and trousers with a blue collar edged with three white tapes and a black kerchief. The cold-weather dress was a blue double-breasted jacket worn over a blue frock and trousers. Headgear included a round blue cap and a sennet hat, sometimes worn with a black cover. This sailor is engaged in the traditional Sunday 'make and mend' session.

D3 Mate, 1849

At the end of the 1846 Navy List was a series of dress regulations, including the order that mates should wear a single right epaulette. Since 1840 mates had worn the same uniform as lieutenants – a double-breasted coat with scarlet collar and cuff-slashes (changed to white in 1843) and a cocked hat with a single gold wire twist loop. The sword had a gilt lion headpiece, white grip, and solid half-basket guard decorated with a crown and anchor. Until 1832 mates had worn a sword with plain pommel and black grip, but were ordered the commissioned officers' pattern in that year. The rank was replaced by that of Sub-Lieutenant in 1861.

E1 Lieutenant, Royal Naval Reserve, 1864

The first regulations governing dress of officers of the reserve appeared in 1864. In undress, as here, the small cap was worn with the distinctive badge of an anchor beneath a crown, encircled with the title 'Royal Naval Reserve'. The cypher 'RNR' appeared on the belt clasp and buttons, and sometimes on the sword hilt and blade. The main difference in the uniforms of active and reserve services was the reserve's use of wavy-lined rank braiding at the cuff. The full dress cocked hat had a waved loop of braid on the right side.

37. 'Monkey jacket' of a Commander, R.N.R., in the inter-war period. Note embroidery on cap peak, and wavy ranking in cuffs. (National Maritime Museum)

38. Battledress of a commander, 1939–45 War. The blue battledress was introduced only in 1943; prior to that date naval officers serving with beach parties wore Army khaki battledress. (National Maritime Museum)

E2 Seaman, landing party, 1882

A member of the landing party which went ashore at Alexandria following the bombardment during Arabi Pasha's revolt. The sennet hat bears the ship's name on the tally band; the blue frock is tucked into the blue trousers, which are confined by black leather gaiters. Belt, braces, pouches and frog are worn in brown leather with steel fittings, together with haversack and canteen. The rifle is the Martini-Henry, with cutlass bayonet.

E3 Assistant Surgeon, 1860

Full dress according to 1856 regulations, in which year a pair of fringeless shoulder-scales replaced the single epaulette previously worn. The 1832 coat has buttons set in threes; Secretarial and Accountant branches had paired buttons, and Navigating branch single spacing. As part of the Civil Branch, this functionary has flat lace on the cocked hat and braid rather than lace on the cuff.

F1 Captain, 1900, No. 4 Dress
The frock coat has five pairs of buttons of which the topmost was to be left unfastened. Ranking is by four bands of lace on the sleeve, the upper band with the 'curl'. The small cap has rank embroidery on the peak. In No. 3 Dress the frock was worn with epaulettes, cocked hat and sword belt.

F2 Lieutenant, Engineering Branch, 1902
This officer, perhaps serving ashore in the Far East, wears No. 8 Dress, a white undress uniform with sun helmet. The helmet has a white *paggri* with a blue band visible at the top edge. The standing-collar tunic has a pocket on the left breast only. The shoulder boards display the branch identifying colour – red – between the lines of ranking lace. In 1905 it became compulsory to wear white shoes with white trousers, except in bad weather ashore; and in 1906 the Wolseley pattern helmet, with wider brim, replaced that illustrated.

F3 Petty Officer, 1899
The khaki service dress worn by the Naval Brigade landed in South Africa for shore duty during the Boer War, 1899–1902. The basic uniform was the Army tunic with stand-and-fall collar, and khaki trousers, with the addition of naval equipment. The sennet hat had a khaki cloth cover with the blue tally band placed over it. Grey canvas gaiters laced up the outer leg in a herringbone pattern. Dark brown leather belt, braces, and pouches were worn; here, the pistol equipment is illustrated, as worn by a Chief Armourer, whose rank is indicated by the badge on the right forearm. Haversack and canteen were carried as required.

G1 Seaman, 1925
This seaman from *HMS Excellent* wears the uniform of the inter-war years; little has changed in a generation. He wears the new Mills Pattern Naval Pistol Equipment adopted in January 1920, with webbing belt, braces, pouch, holster for the .455 Webley & Scott automatic, and frog for the sheathed cutlass. The cutlass was not issued except for ceremonial purposes after 1936, but there are several recorded cases of its being used in action – usually by boarding parties from vessels serving in the East – after the First World War. Webbing leggings were tested at Whale Island in the early 1920s and issued to petty officers and seamen shortly afterwards. This seaman wears three service chevrons in red on the right forearm.

G2 Lieutenant, 1942
An officer as he might appear while serving on North Atlantic escorts in the mid-war years. The 'monkey jacket' is worn over a heavy roll-neck sweater and under the famous 'duffel coat'; heavy seaboots and hose are worn over the uniform trousers. The standard pattern British steel helmet is painted naval grey, with the ranking painted on the front in yellow. The mug of cocoa and the Spam sandwich are not issue items, but were widely observed on the bridge of small warships.

G3 Leading Patrolman, Regulating Branch, 1949
A leading rating of a naval patrol in Malta – a familiar sight to patrons of the sleazier establishments in Valetta. The seaman's hat sports the newly restored white top, abandoned during wartime, and the name *HMS President* on the tally band. The white vest has a distinctive squared neck edged with blue tape, and is worn with white shorts, blue socks, and black shoes. A white webbing belt is worn, and a brassard on the left arm is edged with blue and carries the cypher 'NP' supporting a crown – 'Naval Patrol'. On the left arm is the anchor badge of rank above the two chevrons denoting eight years' service, in blue.

H1 Lieutenant Commander, working dress, 1970
The white-topped cap, now worn in all climates, has a black band, black leather peak, and heavy embroidered badge comprising a crown in heraldic colours above a gold wreath enclosing a silver foul anchor. A white shirt and black tie are worn beneath the dark blue woollen working pullover, which is reinforced at shoulders and elbows with dark blue cloth. Dark blue cloth shoulder straps bear slip-on rank tallies.

39. Ratings loading a Seacat missile launcher on board *HMS Hermione*. Working dress now consists of blue shirts with relevant rank patches on the sleeves and name tallies above the left pocket; blue denim or serge trousers with canvas belts; and black boots or plimsolls. Note anti-flash gloves and hoods. (Crown Copyright)

H2 Seaman, 1970

The combat dress of an ammunition number serving secondary armament; blue work shirt, blue trousers fastened by blue canvas belt with built-in pouch, canvas and rubber plimsoles, and rimless steel helmet. There is a name tab above the shirt pocket. White protective hood and gauntlets are worn against weapon-flash.

H3 Lieutenant, Fleet Air Arm, 1970

The pilot of a Phantom fighter-bomber in full flying kit, with pressure suit, life jacket, and parachute harness in various shades of green and light olive. The 'bone-dome' is white with a darkened plastic visor and attached oxygen mask and tube. Rank tallies are slipped over the shoulder straps of the one-piece suit, and a squadron badge is sewn on a white patch on the right upper arm. The outline of the suit is distorted by numerous pockets and restraints; heavy black ankle-boots are worn.

Légendes

1 'British Plenty' – marin, 1794, en sortie à terre, portant la tenue spéciale, d'une chemise à carreaux, foulard à pois et des chaussures à boucles dorés. 2 Master, en uniforme porté vers 1787 à 1807. 3 Lieutenant, 1799, une gravure Ackerman montre la tenue typique d'un officier subalterne. 4 'Un détachement de la presse' sur Tower Hill à Londres; un dessin humoristique montre les méthodes grossières de recrutement en 1790. 5 Une scène sur le pont principal d'un vaisseau de guerre au port; les femmes réussissaient souvent à monter à bord et les officiers ignoraient cette incartade à la discipline afin de maintenir le moral des hommes. 6 Un pont inférieur de *HMS Victory*, avec les canons, l'équipement, les tables et bancs entre les canons. 7 Un habit-veste de grande tenue de l'Amiral Nelson, avec ses décorations brodées sur la poitrine. A Trafalgar il porta un habit-veste plus simple; voyez la planche **B1**. 8 'La Mort de Nelson' par Dighton, ici on voit beaucoup de détails intéressants de l'uniforme, l'équipement et le fonctionnement des canons. Au centre, se trouve Midshipman Pollock, avec un chapeau d'haute forme, des habits foncés et un fusil; il revindique avoir tiré sur le tireur français qui tua Nelson. 9 Marin de 1807 faisant des sondages avec un fil plombé. Remarquez son chapeau de paille et sa jaquette large, 'frock'. 10 Midshipman 1823, ce lithographe montre la coupe de façon exagérée.

11 Marin qui va être battu au fouet sur le pont d'un vaisseau de guerre. 12 Grand tenue d'un Midshipman, 1827, bien que la coupe ait changé à plusieurs reprises pendant la période, le style de base subsista jusqu'en 1891. 13 Master at Arms ou Quartermaster, vers 1828 un officier contremaître, avec une plaque de couronne et ancre sur sa manche gauche. 14 Captains 1832, le col et les poignets sont écarlates avec des parements dorés. 15 Des volontaires, première classe, et un volontaire deuxième classe, vers 1834, remarquez les chapeaux ronds, les poignets, et parement sur le col. 16 Captain, Flag Officer et Commander en tenues journalières, 1829 – 1833. L'habit-veste de tenue journalière de 1827 est porté ici; notez les parements de rang sur les poignets des personnages à gauche et à droite, et les épaulettes de l'officier général. 17 Le Prince Albert Edouard en uniforme, fait spécialement pour lui par un marin de l'équipe du yacht royal *Victoria and Albert*. 18 Commodore, Captain et Admiral, 1846 à 1856; un fusilier marin et midshipman en arrière plan. Remarquez l'épée de style Mameluc de l'amiral, bien que abolie en 1856, elle fût porté plus tard par certains officiers individuellement. 19 Captain, Lieutenant et Marin, 1846 à 1856, avec un fusilier marin en arrière plan. Aucun règlement ne gouverna la tenue des marins à cette époque, mais un style commun se développa et devint le précurseur de la tenue navale dans la plupart des pays du monde. 20 Marin, 1854. De gauche à droite: Charles Brooks, Admiral's Coxswain, *HMS Britannia*; John Stanley, Boatswain, *HMS Sampson*; Edward Penelly, marin principal, *HMS Sans Pareil*. Remarquez le chapeau goudronné et les blousons à plusieurs boutons.

21 Sir William Peel en uniforme de Capitain, porté pendant la Révolte des Cipayes avec un casque colonial et un dessus en tissus; en arrière-plan, des 'blousons bleus' en chapeaux 'sennet'. 22 Une gravure montrant la tenue de la Marine Royale, les Fusiliers Marins et l'Artillerie Royale de Marines, 1869. 23 Officiers de *HMS Active* en Zoulouland pendant la guerre de 1879. Remarquez les tuniques, guêtres et bandolières de revolvers avec des cartouchières. 24 Brigade Navale, Afrique du Sud, 1879 à 80. Remarquez les dessus en tissus bleu sur les casques des officiers et le dessus sur la casquette d'un marin assis. 25 En arrière plan à gauche. Marins regardant la pendaison des pilleurs à Alexandrie, 1882. Les blousons bleus et chapeaux sennet sont à peine visibles. 26 Captain A. Wilson à la Bataille d'El-Teb, l'uniforme porté par les officiers au Soudan. Wilson fut décoré de la Croix Victoria pour avoir sauvé un de ces hommes, se battant lui-même contre les tribus derviches à coups de poings et la poignée de son épée cassée. 27 Officiers de *HMS Terrible* vers 1890. 28 Marins et fusiliers marins à la distribution des vivres – un officier contremaître pèse la viande. 29 First Class Petty Officer en uniforme 'square rig', vers 1896. 30 Un plongeur marin dans les dernières années du 19e siècle.

31 Le Jour de la Paye, un First Class Petty officer en uniforme blan de tenue légère prend sa paye et la met sur sa casquette; une vieille tradition. 32 Lieutenant en tenue de soirée selon les règlements de 1891. Cette tenue de soirée reste presque inchangée jusqu'à nos jours. 33 Grande tenue d'un amiral, 1904. Remarquez les parements du col, des poignets et la ceinture d'épée. 34 Canon anti-aérien en action à bord d'un vaisseau de guerre pendant la Première Guerre Mondiale. Uniformes bleux, uniformes blancs et des bleus de travail sont portés par cet équipage. 35 Marins regardant La Grande Flotte Allemande en train de se rendre à Scapa Flow, 1918. 36 Marins et Fusiliers marins à Archangel, Russie, 1919. 37 'Jaquette de Singe' d'un Commander, Royal Naval Reserve dans les années 1920 et 1930. Des parements dorés sur le bord du chapeau dénotent le rang, et les lignes ondulées de parement sur le poignet indiquent le Royal Naval Reserve. 38 Le 'battledress' bleu fut introduit comme tenue de travail pendant la Deuxième Guerre Mondiale, ici on voit le rang d'un Commander, indiqué sur les épaulettes. 39 Marins en train de charger une chaloupe à projectile Seacat à bord *HMS Hermione*; ils portent la tenue de travail simple, et des cagoules et gants protecteurs contre des éclairs des armes.

Notes sur les planches en couleurs

A1 Notez que de grands chapeaux ronds étaient portés parfois pour changer; et il n'y avait pas de modèle réglementaire pour les poignards. **A2** Des détails de chapeaux, le type de plaque sur la ceinture etc. étaient laissés au choix de l'individu. **A3** La qualité et les détails des vêtements dépendaient de la distribution de chaque commissaire, qui acheta en gros chez les fabricants. Remarquez les pantalons très larges, 'jupons'.

B1 L'uniforme porté à Trafalgar. Remarquez l'ornement Chelengk en diamants et argent qu'il porta à la place d'une cocarde de chapeau en soie. Il lui fut offert après Aboukir par le Sultan de la Turquie. La visière verte sur le chapeau était un autre détail original. Les médailles sont l'Ordre de la Sicile de Saint Ferdinand et de Valeur; l'Ordre du Bain; l'Ordre Turque du Croissant et l'Ordre Equestre de Saint Joachim de Leiningen. **B2** Les chirurgiens récurent leurs uniformes pour la première fois en juin 1805; ils eurent le même uniforme que celui des médecins mais sans parement doré ou épaulettes, leur rang étant indiqué par la boucle broké sur le col. **B3** (Voir A3 ci-dessus) La qualité et les détails des vêtements dépendaient de la distribution de chaque commissaire, qui acheta en gros chez les fabricants. Des blousons bleus, des gilets de couleurs et des foulards étaient achetés avec la paye de chaque individu. Remarquez la natte goudronnée, très en vogue, et le foulard noir en soie, souvent accroché au front pendant l'action.

C1 Des revers rouges remplacèrent les blancs, cette année, à la demande du Roi William IV. **C2** Cette photo montre la vieille épée de 1805, toujours portée malgré le nouveau modèle de 1827; le modèle de casquette de 1827; et le modèle d'uniforme de 1825. **C3** C'était de coutume de décorer le chapeau goudronné de motifs peints, ayant référence habituellement au nom du vaisseau ou à quelque motif préféré.

D1 Cette photo montre la casquette à visière de 1856 et le modèle d'épée de 1827. **D2** La version de tenue légère du premier uniforme réglementaire officiel pour marins, adopté en janvier 1857. **D3** Une seule épaulette sur l'épaule droite fut adopté par ce rang en 1846. L'épée d'un officier se porta après 1832. Le rang d'un Second (Mate) fut remplacé par celui d'un Sous-Lieutenant en 1861.

E1 En 1864 les premiers règlements apparurent concernant la tenue des officiers de réserve. La marque distinctive fut l'usage de lignes ondulées de galons à la place de parements droits sur les poignets. **E2** Un marin des troupes de débarquement qui se battirent à Alexandrie pendant la révolte du Pasha Arabi, il porte un chapeau sennet avec le galon du vaisseau. L'équipement de l'Infanterie est porté. Le fusil est un Martini-Henry, avec une baionnette sabre. **E3** L'uniforme réglementaire de 1856; cette année là, les contre-épaulettes écarlates sans franges remplacèrent l'épaulette simple portée auparavant.

F1 La rédingote portée sans épaulettes et avec un chapeau rond était 'la Tenue No. 4'. **F2** La rayre rouge sur les bretelles indique l'équipe des mécaniciens. Celle-ci est 'la Tenue no. 8', de la tenue journalière tropicale. **F3** La tenue de service khaki était portée par la Brigade Navale pendant la Guerre des Boers, 1899 à 1902. Un chapeau sennet en khaki est montré ici, avec l'équipement des pistolets et la plaque à la manche d'un Armurier Principal.

G1 Remarquez l'équipement pistolet, Mills Pattern, adopté en 1920, avec un étui pour un pistolet automatique 0.455 Webley et Scott. Des sabres cessèrent d'être fournis aussi tard qu'en 1936, sauf en cas exceptionnel, d'une cérémonie. **G2** Un officier d l'Atlantique du Nord, avec son rang peint sur le devant de son casque, le célèbre manteau 'duffel' et des bottes de marin. **G3** Un Patrouilleur principal de la Naval Patrol à Malte en 1949; observez le brassard 'NP'. Son rang et ses huit ans de service sont indiqués par la plaque et les chevrons · à la manche gauche du gilet à encolure carrée.

H1 Cette photo démontre le pullover bleu en laine porté comme tenue de travail par-dessus la chemise blanche; il a un renforcement en tissus aux épaules et aux coudes. **H2** Tenue de combat comprenant le casque, cagoule et grants protecteurs. Il porte la chemise bleue de travail avec fiche d'identité, pantalons bleus et des chaussures de tennis à semelles en caoutchouc. **H3** Le pilote d'un chasseur Phantom en grande tenue de vol; les plaques de rang song portées sur les bretelles, et la plaque de l'escadron sur le haut de la manche droite.

Überschrift

1 'Britische Fülle' – ein Matrose, 1794, in Urlaubsanzug mit karriertem Hemd, scheckigem Halstuch, vergoldeten Schuhschnallen. **2** Master, in der von 1787–1807 getragener Uniform. **3** Lieutenant, 1799 – eine Zeichnung von Ackermann; typische Oberoffiziersuniform. **4** 'Press Gang' (Zwangsaushebung) zu Tower Hill, London; dieses Spottbild zeigt die groben 'Rekrutierungsmethoden' von 1790. **5** Das Oberdeck eines im Hafenliegenden Kriegsschiffes. Weibe an Bord waren durchaus keine Seltenheiten. Die Offiziere erhoben dagegen oft keine Einspruche, da sie ihre wohltätige Wert zu schätzen wüssten, trotz des Anstosses gegen die Vorschriften. **6** Ein Unterdeck auf *HMS Victory*. Man sieht die Kanonen, das Gerät, die Tische und die Bänke zwischen den Kanonen. **7** Admiral Nelson's Galauniform mit den auf der Brust gestickten Ordensterne. Bei Trafalgar trug er die Alltagsuniform die auf Farbtafel 'B' zu sehen ist. **8** *Nelsons Tod*, nach Dighton. Man sieht viele Einzelheiten über Uniform, Gerät, und die Geschützbedienungsmethoden. In der Bildmitte (hohe Mütze, dunkelen Anzug, Gewehr) steht Midshipman Pollock. Er behauptet er habe den französischen Scharfschützen, der Nelson getroffen hat, getötet. **9** Matrose, 1807, mit der Peileinie. Die Strohmütze und losem Frack bemerken. **10** Midshipman, 1823. Das Bild zeigt die übertriebene Hosenweite.

11 Vollstreckung eine Auspeitschungsstrafe auf einem Kriegsschiff-oberdeck. **12** Galarock eines Midshipmans, 1827. Obwohl über die Jahren leicht geändert, blieb die Grundform bis 1891 behalten. **13** Master at Arms, oder Quartermaster, *c.*1828. Oberste Maatsdienstgrad mit Dienstgradabzeichen (Krone und Anker) am linken Arm. **14** Captains, 1832. Kragen und Aufschläge sind rot mit Goldtressen. **15** Freiwilliger Erste Klasse unter Freiwilliger Zweite Klasse, *c.*1834. Runde Hüte, Dolche und Kragenlitzenschliefe beachten! **16** Lieutenant, Flag Officer und Commander, Interimsuniform, 1829–33. Der Rock ist M1827. Die goldenen Tressen (Dienstgradabzeichen) an den Umschlägen zu den Figuren Links und Rechts, und die Epauletten des Flaggenoffiziers beachten! **17** Prinz Albert Edward (später König Edward VII) in der Uniform der königlichen Yacht *Victoria and Albert*; die Uniform wurde von einem Matrosen angefertigt. **18** Commodore, Captain und Admiral, 1846–56. Im Hintergrund ein Marinesoldat und ein Midshipman. Der Mamelukensabel des Admirals wurde 1856 offiziell abgeschafft, ist aber viel später immer noch getragen worden. **19** Captain, Lieutenant und Matrose, 1846–56. Im Hintergrund ein Marinesoldat. Bekleidungsvorschrift für Matrosen gab es zu dieser Zeit noch night, allgemeine Richtlinien aber waren doch schon vorhanden. Diese bildeten die Basis für Marineuniform über fast die ganze Welt. **20** Matrosen, 1854 – von Links nach Rechts: Charles Brooks, Admiral's Coxswain, *HMS Britannia*; John Stanley, Boatswain, *HMS Sampson*; Edward Penelly, Obermatrose, *HMS Sans Pareil*. Die geteerten Hüte und die reichbeknöpften Jacken beachten.

21 Sir William Peel in Captains Uniform aus der Zeit des indischen Aufstandes, 1857. Er trägt einen mit Stoff überzogenen Weidenhelm. Die 'Blaujacken' im Hintergrund tragen 'Sennet' Hüte. **22** Uniformen der Royal Navy, Royal Marines und Royal Marine Artillery, 1869. **23** Offiziere von *HMS Active* in Zululand während den Krieg 1879. Die Rocke, Gamaschen und die Pistolen-baneliere mit Munitionstaschen beachten! **24** Marine-Brigade, Sud-Afrika, 1879–80. Die dunkelblauen Schützüberzüge auf den Offiziershelme und die Mützenüberzüge des sitzenden Matrosen beachten! **25** Im Hintergrund Links, Einige Matrosen schauen die Hinrichtung Plünderer in Alexandrien, 1882 zu. Die kurzen blauen Jacken und die 'Sennet' Hüte sind gerade sichtbar. **26** Captain A. Wilson in der Schlacht bei El Teb. Er trägt die für Marine Offiziere im Felddienst in den Sudan übliche Uniform. Wilson wurde die Victoria Cross für die Rettung einer seinen Matrosen verliehen. Mit abgebrochener Degenklinge und mit seinen blosen Fäusten kämpfte er für das Leben des Matrosen gegen die anstürmenden Derwischkrieger. **27** Offiziere von *HMS Terrible*, 1890. **28** Matrosen und Marinesoldaten bei der Verpfle-

gungsausgabe. Der Maat weigt den Fleisch aus. **29** First Class Petty Officer in 'square rig' Uniform, *c.*1896. **30** Taucher der Marine – spät 19. Jahrhundert.

31 Geldauszahlungstag. Ein Maat Erste Klasse in weisser Tropenuniform nimmt sein Sold in Empfang und setzt das Geld auf seine Mütze – eine alte Marinesitte. **32** Lieutenant, Ballanzug gemäss Bekleidungsvorschriften von 1891. Dieser Anzug bliebt bis Heute fast unverändert. **33** Die Galauniform eines Admirals, 1904. Zu beachten sind die mit Tressen besetzten Kragen, und Aufschlagpatten und der Degengurtel. **34** Fliegerabwehrkanone eines Schlachtschiffes im Ersten Weltkrieg. Blaue-, weisse-, und Arbeitsuniform sind alle zu sehen. **35** Übergabe der deutschen Hochseeflotte, Scapa Flow, 1918. Die Matrosen schauen zu. **36** Britische Matrosen und Marinesoldaten in Archangel, Russland, 1919. **37** 'Affenjacke' eines Commander, Royal Naval Reserve in den Zwanziger und Dreissiger Jahren. Die Goldtressen an der Mützenkante deuten an den Dienstgrad hin. Die welligen Dienstgradärmeltressen bedeuten Royal Naval Reserve. **38** Die blaue 'Battledress' während dem Zweiten Weltkrieg. Sie wurde als Alltagsuniform eingeführt, hier mit Commanders Dienstgradabzeichen auf den Schulterklappen. **39** Matrosen auf *HMS Hermione* bei der Ladung eines Seacat Raketenwerfers. Sie tragen die einfache Arbeitsuniform, dazu Schützkappen und Schützhandschuhe gegen Waffenblitzwirkung.

Farbtafeln

A1 Hohe, runde Hüte traten auch oft in Erscheinung. Es gab für das Dolchmuster auch keine Vorschriften. **A2** Hutzubehör, Gurtelschnallenmuster und das Aussehen anderer Kleinigkeiten wurden den einzelnen Mann überlassen. **A3** Die Qualität und das Muster der Uniformeinzelheiten hingen vom Schiffszahlmeister ab, der für den Ankauf von Stoff und so weiter von den Herstellerfirmen zuständig war. Zu beachten sind die übervolle Segelstoff 'Unterrockhosen'.

B1 Die Uniform die zu Trafalgar getragen wurde. Die Diamant und Silbernen 'Chelengk' Hutagraffe, die er statt der schwarzseidenen Kokarde trug, is bemerkenswürdig. Sie wurde vom Sultan der Turkei, nach der Schlacht von Aboukir ihm verliehen. Der grune Augenschirm war auch eine persönliche Einführung. Die Ordenssterne sind: St. Ferdinand und Verdienst (Sizilien); Order of the Bath (Gross Britannien); Mondsichelorden (Turkei), der berittene St. Joachimsorden (Leiningen); **B2** Nicht bis 1805 gelangte für Schiffsfeldscherer eine Uniform zur Einführung. Sie war die der Physiker ganz ähnlich, nur statt Goldtressen und Epauletten, trugen die Feldscherer als Dienstgradabzeichen eine Litzenschleife am Kragen. **B3** Vergleich mit Tafel A3. Die Kosten für die blaue Jacke, farbige Weste und Halstuch müsste der Mann selbst bestreiten. Im Einsatz war es üblich, schwarzseidenen Tücher um den Kopf zu binden. Zu beachten ist der beliebten, geteerten Zopf.

C1 Auf besten König William IV wurden in diesem Jahre die Abzeichenfarbe rot statt weiss. **C2** Gezeigt wird der alte Degen M1805; statt der Einführung des neuen Degens M1827, wurde er immer noch getragen. Wir sehen auch die Mütze M1827 und die Uniform M1825. **C3** Es war Sitte, die geteerten Hüte mit Spruche (Schiffsnamen, Treuespruche) zu dekorieren.

D1 Schirmmütze M1856, Degen M1827. **D2** Die erste, vorschriftsmässige Mannschaftstropp-enuniform wurde Januar 1857 eingeführt. **D3** Dienstgradabzeichen für diesen Dienstgrad war seit 1846 die eine Epaulette, rechts getragen. Der Offiziersdegen wurde 1832 erlaubt. Der Dienstgrad 'Mate' wurde 1861 von 'Sub-Lieutenant' ersetzt.

E1 Die ersten Bekleidungsvorschriften für Reserveoffiziere wurden 1864 herausgebracht. Hauptmerkmal sind die wellige statt gerade Armeltressen. **E2** Matrose eines Landungsverbandes der bei Alexandria während Arabi Pashas Aufstand in Einsatz war. Er trägt 'Sennet' Hut mit Schiffsnamenband, Infanteriegestell, Martini-Henry Gewehr mit Entermessebayonet. **E3** Uniform M1856. In diesem Jahre wich die einzige Epaulette dem roten, franzenlosen Schulterschuppen.

F1 'Vierte Uniform'. So hiess der Frack ohne Epauletten und die runde Mütze. **F2** Die roten Schulterklappenstreifen bedeuten 'Schiffsmechanikerabteilung'. Sie werden die 'Achte Uniform' oder 'Troppeninterimsuniform' genannt. **F3** Marine-Brigade im Burenkrieg, 1899–1902. Khaki Dienstanzug mit khakiüberzogenem 'Sennet' Hut. Der Maat trägt Pistole und Gestell; das Armelabzeichen bedeutet 'Chief Armourer' (Waffenschmiedsmeister).

G1 1920 gelangte die der gezeigte 'Mills Pattern' Pistolengestell zur Einführung. Die Pistole ist eine Webley & Scott automatische Waffe. Erst 1936 wurden Entermessen nicht mehr für den Einsatz sondern nur für Paradezwecke herausgegeben. **G2** Marineoffizier, Nordatlantik, mitt Schiffsstiefel und den berühmten 'Duffel Coat'. Auf den Helm ist das Dienstgradabzeichen herangebracht worden. **G3** Unteroffizier einer Naval Patrol, Malta 1949. Der Armband 'NP' beachten. Der Dienstgrad und acht Jahre gute Dienstzeit sind durch Abzeichen und Winkeln auf den linken Arm des eckig ausgeschnittenen Hemdes angezeigt.

H1 Der blaue Arbeitspullover wird über den weissen Hemd getragen. Er hat Verstärkungen aus blauen Stoff an den Schultern und Ellenbogen. **H2** Der Kampfanzug schliesst auch Schützkappe und Schützhandschuhe gegen Waffenblitzwirkung ein. Der Marin trägt blauen Arbeitshemd mit Namensstreife, blaue Hosen und Sportschuhe aus Segelstoff mit Gummisohlen. **H3** 'Phantom' Jagdbomberpilot in voller Ausrüstung. Die Dienstgradabzeichen befinden sich auf den Schulterklappen. Auf den rechten Oberarm ist ein Staffelabzeichen.